George H Dobson

A Pamphlet

George H Dobson

A Pamphlet

ISBN/EAN: 9783743395343

Manufactured in Europe, USA, Canada, Australia, Japa

Cover: Foto ©ninafisch / pixelio.de

Manufactured and distributed by brebook publishing software
(www.brebook.com)

George H Dobson

A Pamphlet

A PAMPHLET

COMPILED AND ISSUED UNDER THE AUSPICES OF THE

BOARDS OF TRADE OF PICTOU AND CAPE BRETON

— ON THE —

COAL INDUSTRY OF THE DOMINION

— ITS RELATION TO THE —

IRON SHIPPING

— AND —

CARRYING TRADE OF CANADA.

BY GEO. H. DOBSON,

SECRETARY, CAPE BRETON BOARD OF TRADE.

PRESENTED TO THE MEMBERS OF PARLIAMENT,
MARCH, 1879.

OTTAWA:
PRINTED BY MACLEAN, ROGER & CO., WELLINGTON STREET.
1879.

CONTENTS.

—

IMPORTANCE OF COAL.

"Coal is entitled to be considered as the mainspring of our civilization. By the power developed in its combustion all the wheels of industry are kept in motion; commerce is carried with rapidity and certainty over all portions of the earth's surface; the useful metals are brought from the deep caves in which they have hidden themselves, and are purified and wrought to serve the purposes of man. By coal, night is, in one sense, converted into day; winter into summer; and the life of man, measured by its fruits, greatly prolonged. Wealth, with all the comforts, the luxuries and the triumphs it brings, are its gifts. Though black, sooty, and often repulsive in its aspects, it is the embodiment of a power more potent than that attributed to the Genii in Oriental tales. Its possession is, therefore, the highest material boon that can be craved by a community or nation.—*Prof. J. T. Newberry.*

"Maritime Provinces."

Says Charles Marshall, in his work, the "*Canadian Dominion*":—

"The Maritime Provinces in confederating with Canada, have augmented its power in a degree immensely exceeding the mere proportion of their population, or extent of their territory.

"They have given her an ample seaboard, thickly studded with excellent harbours, coal-fields nearly as extensive as those of Great Britain, a merchant marine capable of commanding the North American carrying trade, and many thousands of hardy, skilful seafaring men, who, to use the language of Governor Andrews, in his report to Congress on the British North American Provinces, 'from their superior intelligence and bodily vigor, and their experience in the navigation of the cold and stormy coasts, are the best of seamen and well qualified to maintain the honour of their flag on every sea.'"

"'Coal-fields of immense extent occur on the very seaboard (Nova Scotia) to aid the natural advantages of position possessed by the Province for securing the direct trade between the old world and the new."

COAL AND IRON INDUSTRIES OF THE DOMINION

The value of coal, to countries possessing and utilizing it, is made manifest by their prosperity, and the wealth and power of communities and nations whose economy is influenced by its trade or dynamic powers. Of this England furnishes a most prominent illustration. To what can we attribute the astonishing growth of her manufactories, shipping, carrying trade and commerce, but to the development of her immense stores of Coal and Iron? The out-put of her collieries exceeds 130,000,000 tons annually. The 30,000,000 tons used for steam power alone has enabled her to increase her productive ability to equal the work of about 800,000,000 of people, which surpasses in extent, as well as in the multiplicity of its industries, all other countries. This acquisition of mechanical power has enabled her to manufacture for the world and gather wealth from every quarter of the globe.

The out-put of coal for the year 1876 amounted to 135,611,788 tons, which was divided about as follows :—

Purposes for which Used.	Tons.	Percentage of Total Production.
For the iron industry	38,000,000	28·02
Manufacturing purposes	30,000,000	22·11
Domestic use	20,000,000	14·74
Colliery use	9,500,000	7·00
Gas manufacture	7,000,000	5·16
Export	13,000,000	9·58
Railway use	3,750,000	2·76
Steam and navigation	3,650,000	2 68
Lime, cement and salt works	3,400,000	2·57
Chemical works	3,000,000	2·21
Melting metals other than iron	1,000,000	·73
Other purposes	3,311,788	2·44
Total	135,611,788	100 00

The number of hands directly engaged in the mining of this coal was 422,000. Indirectly, however, a very much larger number was employed, inasmuch as the enormous transportation by railways, canals and vessels must be added. At present English coal finds its way to nearly 900 foreign ports ; it crosses all seas and commands nearly every coast, and is used in the interior of countries rich with that mineral.

The stimulating effect of these exports on the commerce of Great Britain is well understood by the nations which attempt to compete with her carrying trade in Europe, America and Australasia.

Prof. Jevons writing on the duration of the English coal supply, remarks: "Coal, in truth, stands not beside, but entirely above all other commodities. It is the material energy of the country, the universal aid, the factor in every thing we do. With coal almost any feat is possible or easy; without it we are thrown back into the laborious poverty of early times." "England's manufacturing, and commercial greatness, at least, is at stake in this question. * * * *. * * To an Englishman who knows the grand and steadfast course his country has pursued to its present point, its future must be a matter of almost personal solicitude and affection."

Next to England in coal production come the United States and Germany.

A writer on American commerce attributes the rapid development of the manufactures and commerce of that country to their immense supply of coal and iron, and a fiscal policy which has led to their development. Since 1821 the coal industry of the United States has enjoyed a protective tariff of from 75 cents to $1.70, and although the coal basins are remote from the sea and not convenient for water or cheap transportation, yet the protective tariff has so secured the home market and increased the out-put of the collieries that the cost of coal mining has been reduced to a minimum. This policy has not only enabled the American coal-owners to compete successfully in foreign markets, but to supply their own consumers as well with cheap coal.

The present out-put of the United States collieries aggregates 50,000,000 tons annually, and gives employment to a working population of over 100,000 people. Prof. James Macfarlane, in his treatise on the American coal trade, remarks: "But unprofitable as it is sometimes to the producer, the public are always benefited by coal-mining. Without following it out in its more remote bearings, its more immediate results are, the distribution among the people, for labor and provisions, of an amount of money equal to the cost of raising and transporting the coal to market, thus affecting the general prosperity of the country. The formation of a home market for all the produce of the country, the employment of numerous tradesmen, merchants, farmers and their families, and the general improvement of all the surrounding country in value and property, are the result. The Anthracite coal alone, mined in 1872, did not cost less than $70,000,000 by the time it was delivered to the customers. All of this money is the result of productive industry, and that sum was added to the wealth of the people. But it would be impossible to describe the vast number of persons, who, directly and indirectly, are indebted to this great interest, not only for the comforts, but the very necessaries of life—food, fuel, raiment and shelter."

The coal fields of the Dominion are said to cover an area of 60,000 square miles, an area more than five times greater than that of the coal fields of Great Britain.

These deposits comprise the anthracite basins of Queen Charlotte Island, British Columbia; the bituminous coal fields of Vancouver, New Brunswick and Nova Scotia, and the lignite deposits in the Saskatchewan, Pembina, Arthabasca and Fraser Rivers.

The coal fields of British Columbia are extensive and rich, their actual area is yet unknown. The coal mines in operation are in the immediate neighbourhood of Nanaimo, Vancouver Island. These collieries are all close to the seaboard, and have every convenience for over sea conveyance, which is the cheapest of all commercial highways for the transportation of bulky articles. The lignite deposits of the interior are situated along navigable streams of great length, affording ready and cheap means of transportation.

But the richest and most important coal fields and collieries of the Dominion are on the Atlantic seaboard, and their development is destined to augment our commerce and carrying trade. The Nova Scotia and Cape Breton coal basins stretch out, under the very water lanes trod by keels in the Canadian and American trans-atlantic trade. The seaboard is ample and studded with excellent harbours, the strata are regular, the coal seams are numerous and easily worked, lying at a moderate angle; each company has its own loading pier and possesses all the conveniences most conducive to working and trading in coal. The annual capacity of the collieries is over 2,000,000 tons or 500,000 tons more than the present consumption of the Dominion, and by reference to the tables annexed, it will be seen that the cost of production in Canada is no greater than it is in England or the United States, while the analysis shows that for gas, steam and domestic purposes our coal is equal to any bituminous coal imported from the United States.

The situation of our mines on the seaboard is pre-eminently adapted for facilitating the carrying trade of the Dominion. Situated on the line of communication between the principal European and North American ports and at the confluence of the St. Lawrence, affording several thousand miles of cheap inland navigation, the development of these collieries will afford return freight for the St. Lawrence, cheapen transportation and vastly expand our commerce.

Our coal and iron deposits extend from the Atlantic to the Pacific; our soil naturally rich can furnish food to almost any extent; our manufactories have a capacity for double their present production; with railways, water routes and shipping which afford every facility for cheap transportation; why are we buying from the United States and England at this moment five times the quantity of coal that we are exporting? Why do we go to England for iron, while our iron resources are more than equal in comparison ? Why do we send from nine to eleven millions of dollars out of the country annually to pay for foreign labour and transportation, increasing foreign markets for foreign commodities, and building up foreign routes of transportation, while our factories are allowed to be idle ? Why do we employ foreigners to do fifty per cent of our carrying trade, while we have a merchant marine only second to that of England and the United States, and a magnificent water course penetrating into the very heart of the Continent, affording every means for cheap transit ? Simply because the products from developed mines and iron factories of other countries are allowed to come in free of duty and crush out our struggling infant industries. The coal mines and iron factories of the Dominion can now supply the demand with as cheap coal and iron as comes from abroad by protecting and securing the home market so as to admit of a large production. Since Confederation we have paid out nearly one hundred million dollars for imported coal and iron, including transportation, while our own mines and vessels lie idle and our workmen are unemployed. Contrast the apathy of our people in reference to these important industries with the energy and interest taken in them by the peoples of the United States, Great Britain, Germany and France, and mark the splendid results to them.

Had we produced the coal and manufactured the iron we would not alone have kept that immense sum of money in the country and experienced the benefit its possession would imply, but would have used it to develop our own mining and manufacturing industries, increased our home market, cheapened the cost of production, placed our mining and manufacturing industries on a sound foundation, developed our carrying trade, and be in position to-day to compete with others in the markets of the world ; but sent to Europe and the United States our capital is lost to us, goes to enrich foreign merchants who receive the benefit, while we experience but the transient heat of the coal and the temporary wearing of the rail.

The money placed in circulation or productive industry added to the wealth of our people by the production of coal and iron, is about as follows, per ton, see tables :-

Money placed in circulation by production per ton	$1 00	
Average cost of transportation from mines to market	2 25	
		$3 25
Cost of production of pig iron	16 88	
Transportation........................	2 00	
		18 88
Cost of bar iron...	43 83	
Transportation.......................................	2 25	
		46 08

It is obvious that every ton of coal imported is $3 lost to our capital, every ton of pig iron $16, and every ton of bar iron is $45 lost to the productive labor of the country.

A fiscal policy is required that will secure the East and West the home market for their respective industries and cause the development of an inter-provincial trade.

The securing of the carrying trade of the West has been the ambition of Canada for many years. To accomplish it millions have been spent in the improvement of the St. Lawrence navigation, which route affords the shortest and most ready means of transit between the granaries of the West and the markets of Europe. Yet with all our natural advantages the American lines are not only holding their own trade but absorbing ours. The large amount of coal tonnage moving west furnishes their routes with return freight, which cheapens transportation and enables them to monopolize the western trade. To compete successfully with the American highways the St. Lawrence requires return freights which can only be afforded by Ontario drawing their supply of coal from our collieries through the St. Lawrence instead of through American channels.

To acquire the Western carrying trade is to acquire wealth and power, and even should the means necessary for its developement cause a temporary advance in our markets, the feeder that the inland commerce would be to maritime trade, and the markets and commerce that would result from its development throughout Canada would more than compensate for any temporary inconvenience the necessary tariff legislation might incur.

DOMINION COLLIERIES.

Description and capacity in tons of the various collieries in the Dominion of Canada, with statistics and evidence given before the Parliamentary Coal Committee, in 1877, on the coal and interprovincial trades.

NOVA SCOTIA MINES.

The following collieries are situated in Pictou County, N.S., are all connected with the interior by the Intercolonial Railway, or can ship from their own wharves in Pictou Harbour or from the Intercolonial wharf at Halifax to any points attainable by water.

ALBION MINES.

JAMES HUDSON, Manager, Stellarton, N.S.

Wharf situate four miles from the town of Pictou, on East River, connecting with the mines by private railway. Depth of water at low tide 18 feet. Capacity 180,000 tons per annum.

Analysis :—

Moisture	1·43	
Volatile combustible matter	26·28	
Fixed carbon	66·50	
Ash	7·74	
		100·00

Cokes well and is largely used for house and steam purposes.

ACADIA MINES.

HENRY POOLE, Manager, Stellarton, N.S.

Wharf on Pictou harbour connecting with mines by private railway, 13 miles in length, connecting with the Intercolonial Railway. Depth of water at low tide 22 feet. Capacity 150,000 tons per annum.

Analysis :—

Moisture .... 2·10
Volatile combustible matter............................. 32·27
Fixed carbon.. 57·57
Ash .... 7·50
Sulphur.. 0·50
                                                    ——— 100·00

Principally used for domestic and steam purposes, considered specially adapted for the latter purpose.

INTERCOLONIAL MINES.

Robert Simpson, Manager, Westville, N. S.

Wharf situate at Middle River, connected to pit by railway seven and a half miles long; distance from wharf to Town of Pictou, three miles ; depth of water at low tide, 19 feet; capacity, 150,000 tons per annumn.

Analysis.

Total volatile matter.. 33·526
Fixed carbon.. 55·390
Ash (grey)... 10·550
Sulphur.. ·594

                                                    100·000

Good for steam and house use. Tried at Pictou Gas Works with following result :—9,500 cubic feet of gas per ton, with 36 bushels of good coke.

VALE COLLIERY.

W. B. Moore, New Glasgow, N. S.

Wharf situate in Pictou harbour, connecting by private railway seven miles in length, with Intercolonial Railway at New Glasgow, thence eight and a half miles to wharf; depth of water at low tide, 26 feet; capacity, 150,000 tons per annum.

Analysis.

Water... 2 22
Volatile combustible matter................................ 30·23
Fixed carbon.. 59·70
Ash (white).. 7·85

                                                    100·000

For a heavy steam coal this mine is unsurpassed, principally used for house and steam purposes. The nut coal from this mine is specially adapted for base burning stoves, &c., being very hard and free from sulphur.

BLACK DIAMOND COLLIERY.

W. W. White, Westville.

Wharf situate on Middle River, connecting with mine by private railway seven and a half miles long; depth of water at low tide, 18 feet; wharf three miles from Town of Pictou; capacity, 80,000 tons per annum. This is the only colliery that does not connect with the Intercolonial Railway. Coal chiefly used for domestic and steam purposes.

SPRINGHILL MINES.

Wm. Hall, Manager, Springhill, N.S.

Situate in Cumberland Co., N.S., connecting by private railway five miles in length, with the Intercolonial Railway but have no facilities for water shipments except from railway docks at Halifax 100 miles away or own wharf at Parsboro on the Bay of Fundy 25 miles away, and Dorchester 40 miles; capacity, 150,000 tons per annum.

Analysis:—

Hygroscopic	1·02
Volatile, combustible matter	34·38
Fixed carbon	60·82
Ash, white	3·78
	100·00

This coal is admirably fitted for the manufacture of gas, yields a compact coke containing but little ash and is well adapted for iron smelting; it is also largely used for domestic and steam purposes.

CAPE BRETON MINES.

The following collieries are situate on the Island of Cape Breton, have at present no railway connection with the mainland but from their location on the Gulf of St. Lawrence command a large supply of seeking ocean tonnage, and have every convenience for cheap transportation to the St. Lawrence, American and West Indian ports.

SYDNEY MINES, C.B.

R. H. Brown, Manager, Sydney Mines, C.B.

Wharves (2 in number) situate on **North Sydney** Harbour connected with mines by railway 4½ miles in length. Depth of water at low tide 25 feet, capacity 200,000 tons per annum.

Analysis :—

Moisture	3·04
Volatile combustible matter	31·14
Fixed carbon	61·50
Ash (reddish brown.)	4·32

100·00

This coal is considered the best domestic coal in Nova Scotia; it is also used for steam purposes.

VICTORIA MINES.

Wm. Routledge, Lessee.

Situated at the entrance of Sydney Harbour. Connected with their wharf by a railway, three miles in length. Depth of water at low tide, 26 feet. Capacity 75,000 tons per annum.

Analysis :—

Volatile matter	38·70
Fixed Carbon	58·40
Ash	2·90

Considered an excellent domestic coal ; is also used for steam.

INTERNATIONAL MINES

International Mine, Dodd and Gillies, Lessees, Sydney, C.B.

Wharf situate on Sydney Harbour connected with mines by private railway, 14 miles in length, depth of water at low tide 30 feet, capacity 150,000 tons per annum.

Analysis :—

Volatile matter	34·09
Fixed carbon	62·92
Ash	2·99

100·00

Admirably adapted for the manufacture of gas, yielding 10,000 cubic feet and 1,470 lbs. of coke per ton ; also used for steam and house purposes.

GARDINER MINE.

WM. ROUTLEDGE, Manager, Bridgeport, C.B.

Situate 10 miles from Sydney Harbour, with which it is connected by the International Coal Co.'s railway, loading vessels also at the latter Co.'s wharf. Depth of water at low tide, 30 feet; capacity, 80,000 tons per annum.

Anaylsis:—

GARDINER.

Volatile matter	31·37
Fixed carbon	64·63
Ash	2·82
Sulphur	1.18

100·00

Is a good house and steam coal specially adapted for the latter purpose.

RESERVE MINES.

Situated 10 miles from Sydney Harbour and 16 miles from Louisburg; connected with both those ports by railway. Depth of water at loading pier at Sydney at low tide, 25 feet. Depth of water at Louisburg pier, 26 feet at low tide.

Capacity 120,000 tons per annum. Regarded an excellent steam and domestic coal.

Analysis :—

Volatile matter	34·50
Fixed Carbon	59·50
Ash	6·00

100·00

Yield of gas per ton, 9,950 cubic feet; illuminating power, 13·17 candles.

EMERY MINES.

Situate near the last named mines; possessing the same railway connection and loading piers at Sydney and Louisburg respectively. The coal of this mine is considered a superior article for steam and smelting purposes. Capacity 80,000 tons per annum.

LINGAN MINE.

R. II. Brown, Manager, Sydney Mines, C.B.

Wharf in Lingan Bay connected with mines by railway three-fourths mi in length. Depth of water at low tide 15 feet, capacity 90,000 tons per annum.

Analysis :—

Volatile matter	33·84
Fixed carbon	63·60
Sulphur	0·77
Ash	1·79
	100·00

Yields 9,700 cubic feet of gas per ton, is also used for steam and house purposes.

LITTLE GLACE BAY MINES.

Charles Rigby, Manager, Little Glace Bay, C.B.

Have excellent harbour for safety at Little Glace Bay. Ship direct from the pit. Depth of water at low tide 18 feet, capacity 120,000 tons per annum.

Analysis :—

Volatile matter	30·21
Fixed carbon	67·78
Ash (reddish brown)	4·32

Yields nearly 10,000 cubic feet of gas per ton, is also largely used for steam and house purposes. Chiefly used for gas.

CALEDONIA MINES.

David Mackeen, Manager, Little Glace Bay, C.B.

Have a good harbour at Port Caledonia, depth of water, 18 feet, connected with the mines by 1 mile of railway, capacity 120,000 tons per annum.

Anaylsis :—

Volatile matter	33·00
Fixed carbon	57·37
Ash	9·63

Is well adapted for the manufacture of gas, yielding 9,700 cubic feet per ton ; also used for house and steam purposes.

ONTARIO MINE.

JOHN SUTHERLAND, Manager, Port Caledonia, C.B.

Ships from the wharf of the Caledonia Mine. Depth of water at low tide 18 feet, capacity 40,000 tons per annum.

Analysis:—

Volatile matter	32·82
Fixed carbon	64·33
Ash	2·85
	100·00

Principally used for steam and house purposes.

BLOCK HOUSE MINING COMPANY.

ROBERT BELLONI, Manager, Cow Bay, C.B.

Situate immediately on the shore of Cow Bay, no railway, depth of water at low tide, 19 feet; capacity, 120,000 tons per annum.

Anaylsis:—

Volatile	35·37
Fixed carbon	59·30
Ash, purplish red	5·33

This coal is peculiarly well adapted for the manufacture of gas, yielding 10,500 cubic feet per ton is also a good steam and house coal, extensively used by the New York Gas Works.

GOWRIE MINES.

CHAS. ARCHIBALD, Manager, Cow Bay, C.B.

Wharf Situate on Cow Bay, connecting with mines by railway 1 mile in length, depth of water at low tide, 19 feet; capacity, 75,000 tons per annum.

Anaylsis:—

Volatile matter	30·64
Fixed carbon	63·00
Ash	3·50
Sulphur	2·86
	100·00

This coal is highly recommended for steam purposes, is a fair domestic coal and produces a superior quality of coke.

TORONTO COAL COMPANY—S. Napier Robinson, Manager.

North Sydney, C.B.

Mine situated on little Bras d'Or Gut. Shipment made direct from pit to vessel. No railway. Depth of water at low tide 20 feet. Capacity 40,000 tons per annum.

Moisture..	1·63
Volatile combustible matter...............................	35·12
Fixed Carbon..	57·19
Sulphur..	trace
Ash...	6·06
	100·00

Considered a good domestic and steam coal, used principally for the former purpose. Vessels loading at this mine for southern ports can proceed to sea through the Bras d'Or Lake, *via* St. Peter's Canal, saving by so doing some eighty miles distance.

NEW CAMPBELLTON MINES.—Hon. C. J. Campbell.

Baddeck, C.B.

Wharf situated one-half mile from mouth of great Bras d'Or, connected with mine by one mile of railway. Depth of water at low tide 23 feet. Capacity, 30,000 tons per annum.

Used for house and steam purposes. Vessels loading here for southern ports can proceed to sea through Bras d'Or Lake and St. Peter's Canal, saving by so doing a considerable distance.

THE BRITISH COLUMBIA COAL MINES.

It has long been known that rich coal deposits exist in British Columbia, and casual statements respecting them have been published from time to time. The latest and most authoritative information is contained in a report of the coal-fields of Vancouver Island, embodied in the recent "Progress Report" and Geological Survey of Canada.

The production of coal in British Columbia was 154,052 tons in 1877, against 139,181 tons in 1876, an increase of nearly 15,000 tons. The mines are on Vancouver Island. The coal of this island is held in high esteem for gas, steam and household purposes. San Francisco is the principal market for its sale.

The following extract is from the report on British Columbia, by Hon. H. L. Langevin, C. B. :—

"The coal-mines of Columbia are very valuable and numerous. The mines of Nanaimo, which yield bituminous coal, are those which, at the present time, are the most worked. They are very easy of access, and vessels can be loaded from them without difficulty. This coal abounds on the eastern coast of Vancouver Island, not only at Nanaimo, but also at Departure Bay, Bayne's Sound, Isquash, and at Moskeeno, near the end of the Island. This coal is, in fact, the only good coal found on the Pacific coast. Mr. Dilke had probably this in his mind when he remarked as follows, in his 'Great Britain': 'The position of the various stores of coal on the Pacific is of extreme importance as an index to the future distribution of power in that part of the world; but it is not enough to know where coal is to be found, without looking also to the quantity, quality and cheapness of labor, and facility of transport. In China, and in Borneo, there are extensive coal fields, but they lie the wrong way for trade. On the other hand, the California coal at Monte Diable, San Diego, and Monterey, lies well, but is bad in quality.'"

The yield of coal in 1869 to 1871, from the Vancouver Coal Mining Company, in British Columbia, was 110,645 tons. The production was 154,052 tons in 1877, against 139,191 in 1876, an increase of nearly 15,000 tons. The coal is held in high esteem for gas, steam, and household purpose. San Francisco is the principal market for its sale.

WELLINGTON MINE.

DUNSMUIR, DIGGLE & Co., Departure Bay, B.C.

Wharves situate on Departure Bay connecting with mines by railway, 3 miles in length; depth of water at low tide, 18 and 25 feet; capacity, 150,000 tons per annum.

Analysis :—

Fixed carbon	55.50
Volatile matter	34.70
Ash	9·80
	100.00

This coal is used principally for steam and domestic purposes.

NANAIMO COLLIERY.

Vancouver Coal Mining Co., Nanaimo, B.C.

Situate at Nanaimo close to the harbour. Depth of water at low tide 24 feet. Capacity 220,000 tons per annum.

Analysis :—

Volatile matter.. 88·05
Fixed carbon................................... .... ,............ 51·45
Ash.. 10 50

Largely used for gas manufacture, also used for steam and domestic purposes.

Anthracite :—

Graham Island, (one of the Queen Charlotte Islands) B.C., Mechanics Institute, New Westminster, B.C.

The deposits of anthracite on the Queen Charlotte Islands are, so far as examined, of very irregular character. The locality best known is on Skidegate Channel, at the southern end of Graham Island. Here the coal has been worked in several places, and found in one instance to be as much as six feet thick. In the direction of its strike, however, it appeared to thin out altogether, or to be represented by coal of very inferior quality mixed with shale and clay iron stone. The seams are vertical, and the rocks containing them are flanked to the north-west by escarpments of volcanic rock.

Analysis of two specimens of the anthracite by fast coking gave (see Report of the Geological Survey of Canada, 1872-73, p. 81) :

Water.	1.99	1.60
Volatile combustible matter..............................	4.77	5.02
Fixed carbon........	85.76	83·09
Sulphur...	0.89	1.53
Ash	6.69	8.76

SHOWING OF THE TABLES.

1. That Nova Scotia exports to the United States have fallen from 465,194 in 1865 to 88,495 tons in 1878, while our importations from the United States have risen from 162,200 tons in 1865, to 746,516 tons in 1878.

2. That the duty in 1870 increased the home production, diminished the importation, and did not increase, but reduced the price to the Dominion consumer.

3. That in the tables annexed, Canada is the only coal producing country in the world which shows a falling off in the output.

4. That with a duty varying from 75 cents to $1.70 per ton on coal, the United States have increased their production from 21,000,000 tons in 1866 to upwards of 50,000,000 tons in 1878, causing with transportation a circulation of not less than 150,000,000 tons of productive capital.

5. That the capacity of the present working collieries of the Dominion is 2,000,000 tons annually; not one-third of this is now being raised to the surface, but with a tariff that would secure the home market, this output would be attained, and the coal delivered to the consumer as cheaply as it could be obtained from abroad.

6. That the analysis shows our bituminous coal for gas, steam or domestic purposes to be quite the equal of any imported from the United States.

7. That the evidence before the coal committee (annexed) shows the position of our coal fields to be such as to secure cheap water transportation with the interior of Canada.

8. That under a protective tariff the production of pig iron in the United States has increased from 1,225,035 tons in 1866, to 2,351,618 in 1878, or 91 per cent., and caused a falling off in the importations of from 215,000 tons = $7,000,000, in 1873, to 67,700 tons in 1877 = $1,000,000.

9. That the importation of railroad iron, including steel rails, has in the United States fallen off from 536,900 tons in 1872 = $22,056,635, to 30 tons $1,464 in 1877.

CANADA FOR CANADIANS.

"A nation, whether it consume its own productions, or with them purchase from abroad, can have no more to spend than it produces. Therefore, the supreme policy of every nation is to develop its own producing forces."

Capital employed in production is spent and yet it reproduces itself. Wherever, therefore, a commodity is produced by the aid of capital, *two capitals* or values are to be regarded. There is first the capital or value spent and consumed in production ; and there is secondly, the capital or value re-produced. It is the capital spent that remunerates the laborer and creates the home market. Yet the country is no poorer for the expenditure in production, for it still has the new made article equivalent or of greater value than the sum spent in production. The country, therefore, that has the resources and privilege of producing at both ends of the exchange has the benefit of spending two consumable capitals instead of one, and double its markets for all other commodities, and in the transaction creates two home markets. But if we produce only one, and leave the foreigner to produce the other, though he should fairly exchange with us, we create but one home market and sacrifice the other.

It is evident that the resources of a young country can only be developed by commanding the home market ; and with our agricultural and manufacturing industries in the west, and minerals and productive interests in the east, a fiscal policy that would secure them the home market would cause an inter-provincial trade which would materially promote the general prosperity of the country.

" The truth is this : —

" The gross value of every product of industry is national net income. Whenever you import instead of producing, you may be losers by the change till your additional export doubles the value of new import."

The west looks to the east for a market for her agricultural and manufacturing industries. The east looks to the west for a market for her minerals and productive industry. The expansion and prosperity of these industries depend on a tariff or fiscal policy that will secure them the home market. Our prosperity is happily interwoven both as agriculturists, manufacturers, miners and carriers with the national prosperity, and we must look for good returns not by seeking to promote special interests or classes of trade, but by seeking the general welfare of the country.

COUNTRIES THAT IMPOSE DUTY ON COAL.

The following countries, although producing no coal within their own borders, levy a duty on all imported :

Cuba, 77 cents per ton.
Barbadoes, 50 cents per ton.

British Guiana, 36c. per ton
Dominica, 50c. "
Antigua, 50c. "
Grenada, 50c. "
Tobago, 50c. "
Trinidad, 75c. "
Bahamas, 17¼c. "
Newfoundland, 25c. "

The following coal producing countries levy a duty on all imported, as follows :

United States, 75 cents per ton.

Germany's new tariff, 5 Pfennings per cwt , which is considered sufficient to shut out English competition, is equal to 25 cents per ton.

France, $1.40 per ton, when carried in other than French bottoms.

" 22c. " when carried in French bottoms.

Spain 25c. "

AMERICAN COAL DUTY AND PRICES.

The following will show the rates of duty imposed upon foreign coal by the United States since 1824, under which protection their coal fields. have been developed, and the wealth of the nation largely increased. From 1854 to 1864 the Reciprocity Treaty was in effect with Canada ; but a duty was on all other foreign coal.

From 1824-32.. $1 00
      18 (3-41 .... 1 32
      1842-47.. 1 70
      1848-54.. 75
      1855-65.. 1 00
      1866-71.. 1 25
      1872-79.. 75

Production of Bituminous coal in Cumberland, U.S., and cost in Boston, during the years 1865-66-67 :

1865, 903,495 tons cost in Boston, $11 00 per ton.
1866, 1,079,331, " 5 94 "
1867, 1,193,822, " 4 97 "

Showing that though a duty of $1.25 was imposed on N.S. coal in 1866, the price fell in the Boston market, from $11.00, in 1865, to $5.94 and to $4.97 in 1867.

TABLE showing comparative value of American, principally imported into Ontario, as compared with Nova Scotia Coals for Steam and Gas purposes.

	Moisture and Vol. Matter.	Fixed Carbon.	Ash.	Sulphur.	Coke in bush. per Ton.	Cubic feet of Gas per Ton.	Candle Power.	Cubic feet of Gas purified by 1 bushel Lime.	Authority.
United States Coals.									
Straitsville	37·25	52·77	9·98	0·68	30 Bush.	10,000	18		Ottawa Gas Co.
Goughoigheny	38·00	56·10	5·90	0·98	30 do	10,000	14		State Geologist, Ohio.
Briar Hill, No. 1	39·50	58·70	1·80	1·15					do
do No. 2	39·80	57·30	2·90	0·76					do
do No. 3	42·73	48·72	8·55						do
Nova Scotia Coals.									
Albion Mine (Picton Co.)	26·76	68·50	7·74	0·55	16·40	9,500	13		Manhattan Gas Co.
Acadia Mine do	34·37	57·57	7·56	0·60					Centennial Report.
Vale Mine do	33·45	59·10	7·85						do
Intercolonial Mine do	33·52	56·39	10·50	0·68					do
Spring Hill Mine (Cumberland Co.)	25·38	60·96	{13·67 / 10·90}	0·84	14·90				Howe and Woodhouse
Blockhouse (O.B.)	40·80	55·70	3·50		14·90	10,217	17	2,304	Manhattan Gas Co.
Phelan do	37·26	54·39	4·35	2·17		9,000	16·5		Manhattan Gas Co.
Emery do	38·10	58·45	3·46			9,500	18		Parcey.
Lingan do	33·84	63·60	1·79	0·79	14·84	9,700	16	1,945	Harrington.
Hub do	36·54	62·53	0·93		14·84	9,566	13		do
Harcob do	34·09	62·92	2·99			10,106	17	2,314	do
Sydney (Min)	31·87	64·59	3·04	2·29	14·40	6,500			Howe.

	Moisture.	Fixed Organic Residue.	Vol. Organic Matter.	Ash.	Sulphur.	
Coke from Albion Mines	0·85	75·80	1·26	22·09	0·297	Steel Co. of Canada.

The sales of the several Collieries in 1876, and Minimum and Maximum capacity, are as follows :—

Name of Colliery and County.	Coal sold in 1876.	Men Employed in 1876.	Min. Capacity.	Max. Capacity.
Cumberland County.	Tons.	No.	Tons.	Tons.
Cumberland Colliery...........	3,096	41	20,000	40,000
Scotia.........	1,121	13	20,000	40,000
South Joggins.........	11,765	64	30,000	60,000
Spring Hill.........	52,395	214	100,000	150,000
Folly Mountain.........	10	....	....	....
Pictou County.				
Acadia.........	45,319	192	100,000	150,000
Albion Mine.........	90,550	615	120,000	180,000
Intercolonial.........	40,622	214	100,000	150,000
Nova Scotia	12,674	85	80,000	120,000
Vale.........	28,365	170	100,000	150,000
Cape Breton.				
Block House.........	31,033	129	80,000	120,000
Caledonia.........	25,323	88	80,000	120,000
Toronto.........	5,693	83	20,000	40,000
Emery.........	40	14	40,000	80,000
Gardiner.........	....	5	40,000	80,000
Glace Bay.........	28,598	127	80,000	120,000
Gowrie.........	20,103	166	50,000	75,000
Ingraham.........	40	....	....	....
International.........	24,111	109	100,000	150,000
Lingan.........	15,289	103	60,000	90,000
Ontario.........	11,096	75	20,000	40,000
Reserve.........	....	10	80,000	120,000
Schooner Pond.........	....	20	40,000	60,000
South Head.........	653	11	20,000	30,000
Sydney Mines.........	102,644	516	150,000	200,000
Victoria.........	17,672	90	50,000	75,000
Port Hood.........	2,548	27	20,000	30,000
New Campbellton.........	3,362	48	20,000	30,000
British Columbia.				
Bayne's Sound Colliery.........	1,000	} 441	{ 20,000	30,000
Wellington.........	60,000		100,000	150,000
Nanaimo.........	150,000		200,000	230,000
Totals	**785,121**	**3,770**	**1,940,000**	**2,900,000**

COAL Sales in Nova Scotia from 1785 to 1875 (Inclusive).

Year.	Sales.	Total.	Year.	Sales.	Total.
1785	1,668		1831	37,170	
1786	2,000		1832	50,396	
1787			1833	64,743	
1788	10,681		1834	50,813	
1789			1835	56,434	
1790			1836	107,593	
		14,349	1837	118,942	
			1838	106,730	
1791	2,670		1839	145,962	
1792	2,143		1840	101,198	839,961
1793	1,926				
1794	4,405		1841	148,298	
1795	5,320		1842	120,708	
1796	5,249		1843	105,161	
1797	6,039		1844	108,482	
1798	5,948		1845	150,674	
1799	8,947		1846	147,506	
1800	8,401		1847	201,820	
		51,048	1848	187,643	
			1849	174,502	
1801	5,775		1850	180,084	
1802	7,769				1,533,798
1803	6,601				
1804	5,976		1851	153,499	
1805	10,130		1852	189,076	
1806	4,938		1853	217,426	
1807	5,119		1854	234,312	
1808	6,616		1855	238,215	
1809	5,919		1856	253,492	
1810	6,609		1857	294,198	
		70,452	1858	226,725	
			1859	270,293	
1811	8,516		1860	322,593	
1812	9,570				2,399,829
1813	9,744				
1814	8,866		1861	326,429	
1815	9,336		1862	395,637	
1816	8,619		1863	429,351	
1817	9,284		1864	576,935	
1818	7,920		1865	635,586	
1819	8,692		1866	558,520	
1820	9,980		1867	471,195	
		91,527	1868	453,624	
			1869	513,795	
1821	11,388		1870	568,277	
1822	7,512				4,927,329
1823					
1824	27,000		1871	596,418	
1825			1872	785,914	
1826	12,600		1873	881,108	
1827	12,149		1874	749,127	
1828	20,967		1875	706,795	
1829	21,935		1876	634,207	
1830	27,280		1877	687,065	
		140,820	1878	893,511	
					5,734,143
			Total		15,803,368

NOVA SCOTIA COAL SALES, HOME AND FOREIGN.

Provinces.	1866.	1867.	1868.	1869.	1870.	1871.	1872.	1873.	1874.	1875.	1876.	1877.	1878.
Quebec	9,600	12,206	9,191	4,419				187,059	162,209	189,754	117,303	95,118	83,710
New Brunswick					21,452			68,217	78,841	85,988	101,890	104,818	115,249
Newfoundland					40,699			53,861	55,696	62,348	51,742	49,342	61,391
Prince Edward Island								26,640	41,948	43,641	46,908	45,169	43,412
Nova Scotia						252,170	154,092	215,295	214,965	212,630	225,636	255,790	279,172
United States	404,252	338,492	198,920	376,135	209,448			264,760	138,335	89,746	71,634	118,216	88,496
West Indies			820		1,170	1,380		54,213	47,844	16,429	17,971	12,660	16,999
East Indies										1,003			
South America			147	188	120	60		1,885	5,077	4,779		573	535
French West Indies					2,305	1,551							
Spanish West Indies			4,311	3,407	10,211	2,879							
Spain					69	190							
St. Pierre et Miquelon			2,689	2,330	2,699	3,302							
Great Britain			666	200	170	270		6,976	4,152		1,101	4,379	3,694

Exports of Coal into the United States from Nova Scotia.

Year.	Tons.	Duty.	Year.	Tons.	Duty.
1850	98,173	24 ad val.	1865	465,194	Reciprocity.
1851	116,274	do	1866	404,252	$1 25
1852	87,542	do	1867	338,493	1 25
1853	120,764	do	1868	228,132	1 25
1854	139,125	Reciprocity.	1869	257,485	1 25
1855	103,232	do	1870	168,180	1 25
1856	126,152	do	1871	165,431	1 25
1877	123,335	do	1872	151,092	0 75
1858	186,743	do	1873	264,760	0 75
1859	122,720	do	1874	138,335	0 75
1860	149,289	do	1875	89,746	0 75
1861	204,457	do	1876	71,634	0 75
1862	192,612	do	1877	116,210	0 75
1863	282,774	do	1878	88,495	0 75
1864	347,594	do			

Imports of Coal into Canada from the United States (from Canadian Blue Books.)

Year.	No. of Tons.	Year.	No. of Tons.	Remarks.
1860	79,886	1873	463,858	
1861	171,561	1874	671,023	
1862	105,905	1875	512,835	
1863	103,547	1876	625,203	
1864 (six months)	22,100	1877 {	415,869	Anthracite.
1865	132,200		353,795	Bituminous.
1866	110,755			
1867	282,669		769,664	
1868	183,591			
1869	204,268	1878 {	404,389	Anthracite.
1870	222,614		342,127	Bituminous.
1871	165,350			
1872	311,091		746,516	

IMPORTS OF COAL INTO CANADA.

Provinces.	Great Britain.		United States.		Nova Scotia.		Total Tons.	Total Value.
	No. of Tons.	Value.	No. of Tons.	Value.	No. of Tons.	Value.		
		$		$		$		$
1860 { Ontario .... / Quebec		275,663	79,886	304,072		360	194,545	592,464
1861, Canada (proper).		266,329	171,561	458,665		12,323	245,961	733,211
1862, do		330,410	105,905	437,391		7,318	239,728	781,865
1863, do six months		379,703	103,547	548,846		760	239,394	934,329
1864, do		96,084	22,100	96,031		13,294	58,049	185,477
1865, do		463,476	132,200	544,611		7,690	264,665	1,036,198
1866, do		419,847	110,754	485,690		3,362	220,276	906,700
1867	108,561	472,710	182,660	790,476	9,600	21,170	299,507	1,253,116
1868	104,634	539,606	183,391	791,998	12,206	30,003	353,873	1,263,527
1869	161,291	540,568	204,968	847,329	9,191	48,834	387,243	1,386,785
1870	178,555	531,098	213,614	921,044	4,419	31,366	420,390	1,465,742
1871	197,776	272,085	165,350	749,805		10,888	272,665	1,031,890
1872	107,245	639,849	311,091	1,375,384	Other Countries		484,819	2,015,233
1873	173,726	592,738	463,868	1,983,981	205	1,070	574,167	2,557,789
1874	110,104	723,708	671,023	3,079,652			804,414	3,065,290
1875	133,391	551,377	512,635	2,624,771			652,435	3,075,088
1876	139,600	494,958	635,303	2,524,975	35	127	793,680	3,320,060
	168,842							
1877 { Anthracite ..... / Bituminous...........	4,011 / 160,175	15,693 / 401,644	415,869 / 353,795	1,777,439 / 1,304,510			933,980	3,499,561
Totals......	161,186	412,337	769,664	3,085,149		2,179,257		
Ontario.								
1878, Anthracite ..... / do Bituminous			266,432 / 327,384	1,026,816 / 1,153,441				

Quebec.						
1876, Anthracite	2,533	7,303	105,384	333,836		
do Bituminous	121,560	315,299	7,783	31,120		
do Other coal	17,728	39,168	1,637	6,776	732,393	894,796
Other Provinces.						
1876, Anthracite	3,074	7,765	32,573	107,..1		
do Bituminous	6,949	17,728	5,433	21,970		
do Other coal						
Totals, 1876	151,833	387,364	746,616	2,680,639		3,064,846

Iron Production of the Globe, 1866 to 1877.

Countries.	Production.				Percentage of Increase.
	Year.	Tons.	Year.	Tons.	
Great Britain	1866	4,596,279	1876	6,660,893	44 92
Germany....................................	1866	1,000,492	1876	1,614,687	61·38
France	1866	1,260,346	1877	1,453,112	15·30
Belgium....................................	1866	482,404	1876	490,508	1·68
Russia	1866	314,850	1875	426,896	35·59
Austro-Hungary	1866	284,636	1876	400,426	40·68
Sweden....................................	1866	230,670	1876	351,718	52·48
Luxemburg	1866	46,460	1876	231,658	398·62
Spain......................................	1866	39,254	1873	42,825	8·92
Italy......................................	1866	22,200	1875	20,278	....
Other Countries of Europe................	....	....	1876	60,000	....
United States	1866	1,225,031	1877	2,351,618	91·96
Other Countries of America...............	....	....	....	115,000	....
Asia.......................................	....	....	....	60,000	....
Africa.....................................	....	....	....	30,000	....
Australia..................................	....	....	....	15,000	....
Canada....................................	....	....	1877	11,000	....
Total	....	14,324,619	....	14,335,619	....

COAL Production of the Globe, 1866 to 1877.

Countries.	Production.				Per-centage of Increase	Per-centage of Decrease
	Year.	Tons.	Year.	Tons.		
Great Britain	1866	103,060,804	1876	135,611,786	31·57	
Germany	1866	28,162,805	1877	48,296,367	71·48	
France	1866	12,234,455	1877	16,889,201	38·04	
Belgium	1866	12,774,662	1876	14,329,578	12·17	
Austro-Hungary	1866	4,893,933	1876	13,362,586	175·08	
Russia	1866	271,533	1875	1,709,269	529·49	
Spain	1866	432,664	1876	706,814	63·36	
Italy	1866	70,009	1875	102,140	45·91	
Sweden	1866	36,467	1876	92,352	153·25	
Other Countries of Europe				80,000		
United States	1866	21,856,844	1875	48,273,447	120·85	
Canada	1866	558,519	1876	709,646	27·06	
Other Countries of America	?			400,000		
Asia				4,120,000		
Africa				100,000		
Australia	1866	774,000	1876	1,380,000	78·29	
Canada (N.S. and B.O.)	1873	1,150,467	1877	927,426		19·38
Total		186,266,153		287,090,604		

AMERICAN PRODUCTION OF PIG IRON FROM 1854 TO 1877.

In the following table we give the statistics of the production of pig iron in the United States from 1854 to 1877, classified according to the kind of fuel used.

Years.	Anthracite.	Charcoal.	Bituminous Coal and Coke.	Total.
1854	339,435	342,298	54,485	736,218
1855	381,866	339,922	62,300	784,178
1856	443,113	370,470	69,554	883,137
18..	390,385	330,321	77,451	798,157
1858	361,430	285,313	58,351	705,094
1859	471,745	284,041	84,841	840,627
1860	519,211	278,331	122,228	919,770
1861	409,229	195,278	127,037	731,544
1862	470,315	186,660	130,697	787,662
1863	577,638	212,005	157,961	947,604
1864	684,018	241,853	210,125	1,135,996
1865	479,558	262,342	189,662	931,582
1866	749,367	332,580	268,396	1,350,343
1867	798,638	344,341	318,647	1,461,626
1868	893,000	370,000	340,000	1,603,000
1869	971,150	392,150	553,341	1,916,641
1870	930,000	365,000	570,000	1,865,000
1871	956,608	385,000	570,000	1,911,608
1872	1,369,812	500,587	984,159	2,854,558
1873	1,312,754	577,620	977,904	2,868,278
1874	1,202,144	576,557	910,712	2,689,413
1875	908,046	410,990	947,545	2,266,581
1876	794,578	308,649	990,009	2,093,236
1877	934,797	317,843	1,061,945	2,314,585

AMERICAN IMPORTATION OF IRON.

QUANTITIES and Value of Pig and Rolled Iron imported into the United States from 1855 to 1877, compiled from Statistics supplied by the United States Bureau of Statistics.

Fiscal Years.	Pig Iron.		Railroad Iron, Including Steel Rails.		Bar, Rod, Hoop, Sheet and Plate Iron.	
	Gross Tons.	Value.	Gross Tons.	Value.	Gross Tons.	Value.
		$		$		$
1855.	98,925	1,979,463	127,510	4,993,900	144,911	7,728,406
1856.	59,012	1,171,185	155,495	6,179,260	187,778	6,990,744
1857.	51,794	1,001,742	170,905	7,455,596	123,970	6,640,900
1858.	41,086	730,940	75,745	2,987,576	91,546	4,963,811
1859.	72,517	1,049,200	60,965	2,274,032	120,686	5,657,305
1860.	71,498	1,005,865	122,175	3,700,376	172,532	6,407,738
1861.	74,020	979,916	74,490	2,162,605	125,454	5,585,496
1862.	22,247	285,323	8,611	222,967	33,170	1,581,270
1863.	31,007	435,194	17,088	540,494	86,834	4,102,227
1864.	102,223	1,288,424	118,714	3,904,017	123,830	5,981,150
1865.	50,052	806,552	77,618	2,903,826	65,292	3,740,855
1866.	102,392	1,083,186	78,007	2,806,390	79,926	3,993,356
1867.	112,042	1,831,465	96,272	3,317,862	101,754	5,335,665
1868.	112,133	1,778,977	151,097	4,373,162	92,350	4,788,012
1869.	136,975	2,136,030	237,703	7,306,845	102,701	4,945,910
1870.	153,283	2,509,280	270,765	9,669,571	89,370	4,479,524
1871.	178,138	3,106,490	458,055	17,360,297	112,735	5,306,720
1872.	247,528	5,122,318	531,536	22,086,835	130,200	6,900,521
1873.	215,495	7,203,769	357,629	19,740,702	95,744	7,477,556
1874.	92,041	3,288,023	148,918	10,758,435	40,103	4,042,078
1875.	53,748	1,455,668	42,082	2,932,311	28,929	2,813,854
1876.	79,455	1,918,547	4,708	321,020	30,898	2,317,125
1877.	67,922	1,556,415	30	1,464	26,306	1,632,815

The production of anthracite pig iron first overtook that of charcoal in 1855, and the production of bituminous coal and coke pig iron first overtook that of charcoal in 1869 and that of anthracite in 1875.

PRICES OF AMERICAN BITUMINOUS COAL.

AVERAGE Price in Dollars of Cumberland Coal, F. O. B. at Baltimore, from 1853 to 1878, with Average Freight to Boston—Per ton of 2,240 lbs.

Years.	January.	February.	March.	April.	May.	June.	July.	August.	Septemb'r	October.	Novemb'r.	December.	Average for year.	Average freight to Boston.	Average cost d'v'd at Boston.
	$ c.	$ c	$ c.	$ c.	$ c.	$ c.	$ c.	$ c.	$ c.	$ c.	$ c.	$ c.	$ c.	$ cts.	$ cts.
1853...........	......	...	......	......	3 15	......	3 15	3 15	......	3 15	3 62	3 50	......	2 80	......
1854...........	3 50	......	......	......	......	......	......	4 00	4 25	......	4 25	4 25	......	2 25	......
1855...........	4 25	4 25	4 25	4 00	3 75	3 75	3 75	3 75	3 75	3 75	3 75	3 75	3 89	2 17	6 06
1856...........	......	......	3 75	3 75	3 75	3 75	3 75	3 75	3 75	3 75	3 75	......	3 75	2 37	6 12
1857...........	4 35	4 35	4 35	4 50	4 28	4 24	4 23	4 15	4 23	4 25	4 25	4 25	4 28	1 84	6 12
1858...........	......	...	3 80	3 75	3 50	3 73	3 62	3 75	3 63	3 75	3 75	3 75	3 70	1 73	5 43
1859...........	4 12	3 75	3 37	3 18	4 07	3 65	3 45	3 93	3 43	3 55	3 55	3 55	3 63	1 83	5 46
1860...........		3 50	3 75	3 45	3 37	3 60	......	......	......	3 50	3 25	3 50	3 47	2 55	6 02
1861...........	3 00	3 66	3 43	3 50	3 50	3 50	3 50	......	...	......	......		3 44	2 25	5 69
1862...........	......	......	4 00	4 00	4 25	4 11	4 33	4 25	......				4 16	2 43	6 58
1863...........	5 50	6 00	6 00	5 06	5 50	5 50	5 50	5 50	5 50	5 25	5 50	5 50	5 57	3 28	8 85
1864...........	5 75	5 75	5 83	6 00	6 14	6 21	......	7 41	......	8 36	8 36	8 63	6 84	3 39	10 23
1865...........	8 56	......	10 25	9 01	8 00	6 50	6 75	7 00	7 00	6 75	6 75	6 75	7 57	3 79	11 36
1866...........	6 35	7 00	6 00	6 00	6 00	6 00	5 75	5 66	5 63	5 66	5 62	5 66	5 94	3 53	9 47
1867...........	......	......	5 25	5 13	5 08	4 88	4 82	4 86	4 92	4 88	4 86	4 88	4 97	2 68	7 65
1868...........	5 00	5 00	4 87	4 75	4 70	4 70	4 68	4 67	4 70	4 75	4 83	4 83	4 79	3 21	8 00
1869...........	5 00	5 00	5 00	4 96	4 96	4 96	4 96	4 96	4 96	5 00	5 00	4 96	4 97	2 83	7 80
1870...........	4 72	4 72	4 72	4 72	4 72	4 72	4 72	4 72	4 72	4 72	4 72	......	4 72	2 64	7 36
1871...........	4 72	4 72	4 72	4 72	4 72	4 72	4 72	4 72	4 72	4 72	......	4 72	4 72	2 73	7 45
1872...........	4 70	4 65	4 82	4 64	4 64	4 64	4 64	4 64	4 64	4 75	4 75	......	4 66	3 06	7 72
1873...........	4 75	4 75	4 83	4 93	4 93	4 85	4 85	4 85	4 88	4 88	......	......	4 85	3 05	7 90
1874...........	4 65	4 63	4 65	4 65	4 65	4 65	4 55	4 55	4 65	4 65	4 65	4 65	4 63	2 28	6 91
1875...........	4 65	4 70	4 35	4 40	4 40	4 30	4 30	4 30	4 40	4 40	4 40		4 42	2 11	6 53
1876...........	4 25	4 20	4 00	3 90	3 90	3 85	3 85	3 75	3 90	3 85	3 90	3 80	3 93	1 83	5 76
1877...........	3 72	3 80	3 78	3 33	3 20	3 20	3 20	3 20	3 16	3 17	3 17	3 17	3 34	1 70	5 04
1878...........	3 17	3 17	3 17	3 17	3 06	......	......	......	......	......	......	......	3 15	1 50	4 65

Estimated area of the coal deposits of the different countries of the world :—

	Square Miles.
United States	192,000
Canada	60,000
Russia	30,000
Australia	24,000
Great Britain	11,900
Japan	5,000
Spain	3,501
France	2,086
India	2,004
Germany	1,770
Belgium	510

THE COST OF PRODUCING COAL.

A comparison of the expenses in the working of collieries will show how favourably the cost of mining in Canada compares with that of other countries.

Cost of Mining in England.

The following gives the actual cost in detail as it was early in 1878 :—

	Durham. Cts.	Northumberland. Cts.
Heaving	36	52
Other underground labor	30	30
Outside labor	17½	17
Royalty	11½	12
Materials, horses, machinery	24	23
Taxes and office charges	04	05
	$1 23	$1 40

Cost of American Coal.

These figures show the out-put of the Blossburg Bituminous Coal Mines, Pa., in 1877, the pay-roll for the year, and its cost per ton :—Coal raised, 182,707 tons ; pay-roll of the mines for the year, $186,000 ; cost of coal, $1.02.

The average cost of production for the 26 Bituminous Collieries in the County of Allegheny, in 1877, by the pay-roll of the mines, was 99 cents per ton.

3

Cost of Nova Scotia Coal.

The following is the out-put of the Glace Bay Mines, C.B., Nova Scotia, in 1877, and the cost of the production by the pay-roll:—Coal raised, 35,000 tons ; pay-roll for the year, $33,600 ; cost per ton, 95 cents.

Cost of American Anthracite.

The following figures gives the out-put for a series of years, and shows the effect of large production in the cost, tonnage, expenses, and average cost per ton for coal at collieries worked by the Philadelphia and Reading Coal and Iron Company :

Years.	. Tons.	Expenses.	Cost per Ton.
1873.............	1,348,838	$3,385,149 68	$2 51
1874.............	1,374,790	3,364,908 37	2 44·8
1875..........	1,510,572	2,821,609 51	1 86·7
1876..........	1,835,364	2,509,483 34	1 35·4
1877..........	3,794,528	3,942,591 71	1 09·9

To show more fully how ' ·gely production governs the cost of mining. The out-put of the above mines in April, 1875, was 5,790 tons; the cost per ton for that month, $12.53.

In November of the same year the out-put was 228,895 tons, and cost per ton only $1.60.

In February, 1877, the out-put was 133,114 tons, and the cost per ton $1.72.

In November of the same year the production came up to 279,247 tons, and the cost declined to 85 cents per ton.

These estimates do not include interest on capital invested or the royalty (except of the English mines), nor the depreciation of the plant.

COST OF PRODUCTION OF IRON IN U. S.

AVERAGE Cost per Ton of Pig Iron on Furnace Bank, and of Merchant Bar in Mill, from 1875 to 1879, inclusive, compiled from original data by Mr. W. E. S. Baker, Secretary of the Eastern Ironmasters' Association.

AVERAGE COST OF PIG IRON, 1875 TO 1879.

	1875.	1876.	1877.	Jaunary, 1879.
	$ cts.	$ cts.	$ cts.	$ cts.
Cost of Ore to the ton of Pig Iron............	11 95	9 54	7 69	6 51
do Coal do	8 01	6 79	4 93	5 29
do Limestone do	1 14	1 01	0 81	0 78
do Labour do	2 97	2 54	2 02	1 86
do General contingencies	2 10	1 73	1 65	1 29
Cost at Furnace Bank.......	26 17	21 61	17 10	15 73
Add interest on capital on a product of 6,000 tons.	1 70	1 59	1 26	1 15
Total cost to the producer................	27 87	23 20	18 36	16 88

AVERAGE COST OF BAR IRON, 1875 TO 1879.

	1875.	1876.	1877.	January, 1879.
	$ cts.	$ cts.	$ cts.	$ cts.
Cost of Pig Iron to the ton of Finished Bar Iron...	29 12	25 19	21 93	20 13
do Coal do do ...	8 73	6 85	5 89	6 01
do Labour ... do do ...	16 87	15 74	12 93	11 98
General contingencies...........	4 79	4 73	4 62	4 41
Cost in the Mill, finished	59 51	52 51	45 37	42 53
Add interest on capital on a product of 6,000 tons.	1 86	1 70	1.35	1 30
Total cost to the Manufacturer..........	61 37	54 21	46 72	43 83

	Tons.	Cwt.	Qrs.	Lbs.
Quantity of Ore used to make one ton of Pig Iron, average 10 years	2	15	1	17
do Coal do do do ...	1	14	3	27
do Limestone do do do ...	....	16	1	06

The above group of furnaces used Juniata and Montour hematite ores, and a little Cornwall. The coal came chiefly from the Lehigh and Wyoming Valleys.

AVERAGE COST OF BAR IRON, 1875 TO 1879—*Concluded.*

—	Tons.	Cwt.	Qrs.	Lbs.
Quantity of Pig Iron used to make one ton of Finished Bar Iron, average 10 years.	1	04	1	13
Quantity of Coal used to make one ton of Finished Bar Iron, average 10 years	1	12	2	03

The above rolling-mills used Gray Forge pig iron and Clearfield and Cumberland coal.

COAL EXPORTS OF GREAT BRITAIN.

The following table will show the export coal trade of the United Kingdom, and the countries to which exported, omitting those taking less than 50,000 tons.

Countries to which Exported.	Tons. 1877	Countries to which Exported.	Tons. 1877.
Northern ports of Russia.........	943,584	Algeria...........................	60,720
Southern ports of Russia.........	85,319	West Coast of Africa...........	88,636
Sweden	775,284	British South Africa..........	55,916
Norway..........................	438,875	Continental India.............	577,337
Denmark......	765,608	Straits Settlements	222,509
Germany.............................2,042,911		Ceylon.............................	96,117
Holland...............	411,555	Java..	111,533
Belgium	259,257	China.............................	119,254
Channel Islands....................	66,552	British North America..........	179,076
France............................:.....3,010,143		United States—Atlantic Coast..	63,136
Portugal, Azores and Madeira .	260,293	do Pacific Coast....	75,378
Spain and Canaries..............	826,471	British West Indies..............	173,992
Gibraltar...........................	180,522	Foreign West Indies..............	286,580
Italy 1,072,928		Peru..................................	84,093
Austrian Territories..............	82,943	Chili..................................	160,460
Malta.	278,211	Brazil ......,.......................	340,225
Greece.	80,578	Uruguay.............................	141,404
Turkey..........................	217,991	Argentine Republic	59,175
Egypt.....................	520,476		

COAL EXPORTS OF UNITED STATES.

The following shows the export trade of the United States with the West Indies and South America for 1877 :—

Countries.	Tons Bituminous.	Tons Anthracite.
Brazil..	115	466
Central American States......	59	61
Chili.	1,940	1,021
Danish West Indies	7,779	......
French West Indies..............................	3,424	175
British West Indies	1,693	2,093
Dutch West Indies.................................	......	202
Peru.....................	......	2,138
San Domingo..	297	484
Cuba...	55,168	17,342
Porto Rico	......	347
U. S. of Columbia..................................	19,967	3,320
Venezuela..	1,543	216

PRICE COAL AT TORONTO.

March 1st, 1879, prepared by Rogers & Co., of Toronto, for this Pamphlet.

Names and prices of the principal coals at present used in Toronto, coming from the United States :—

Brookfield	$4 27	per ton of 2.000 lbs.
Churchill	4 27	do
Best Briar Hill	4 27	do
Union Briar Hill..............................	3 97	do
Massilon.................................	3 47	do
Straitsville..	3 47	do
Monday Creek.......	3 47	do
Youghoigheny........................	4 00	do
Reynoldsville...	3 90	do

Extract from letters of Mr. H. A. Budden, Montreal, read before the Dominion Board of

Trade, 17th January, 1878.

MONTREAL, 13th December, 1877.

Among the various industries of the Dominion, that of coal mining is destined to take a prominent and exert an influence second to none. Canada will not attain its proper position until its extremities are bound together by a trans-continental railway, and traffic from the Atlantic and Pacific Oceans carried over it, the motive-power, coal, lies in abundance. The Nova Scotia collieries have been worked since 1785, while those of Vancouver Island are only in their infancy. No other fields have yet been opened; the total product of Vancouver Island in 1876 was about 150,000 tons, principal amount going to San Francisco. The quality of coal is very similar to that of Nova Scotia. The collieries are all situated near the sea, and capable of indefinite extension. The Nova Scotia coal fields, stretching out as they do into the Atlantic Ocean, invite the commerce of the world, and furnish coal at a nearer point to the sea board than any coal fields of the United States. On the Island of Cape Breton the coal area is very extensive and the coal of excellent quality, much esteemed for gas making and other purposes. North Sydney is becoming an important port of call for vessels seeking cargo, not only from the St. Lawrence, but from all ports on the Atlantic sea board. The collieries delivering coal in Sydney Harbour can supply an unlimited amount

The Pictou coal field is on the mainland of Nova Scotia, and within a few miles of Pictou Harbour, being also connected with Halifax by rail, one hundred miles distant. Five collieries are in operation fully equipped but languishing for want of demand; the excellent quality of those coals renders their use available for every purpose—they are exceptionally free from sulphur, and make a coke equal to the best North Durham; their hardness and exceptional freedom from foreign substances make them safe for shipment to warm climates. The Maritime Provinces with their fishing, shipping and mineral wealth will afford a growing market to the agriculturalists of Ontario and the west. Quebec will naturally take a foremost position in manufactures, and draw supplies from all. Ontario, besides her agriculture, has her petroleum wells and salt to develop. To enlarge the home market for coal and iron, a moderate tariff is required sufficient to give an impetus to their production and manufacture. This necessity arises from the peculiar position of Canada, her present home market is limited, and the miners and manufacturers of Great Britain and the United States are eager to control it.

The peninsula of western Ontario can have no cause to complain of a moderate tariff on coal and iron; the products, breadstuffs, cattle, butter, cheese and petroleum will find an increasing demand from a growing population in the Maritime Provinces.

An increased production of coal will enable it to be produced at a very much lower cost, and there is no reason why it should not compete with American coal on Lake Ontario, and neutralize the effect of the proposed duty.

An important feature in the improvement of the coal trade would be the establishment of sugar refineries at Halifax, St. John and Montreal and other places not only would the consumption of coal as fuel be considerable, but the export demand for coal as return cargo to the West Indies, and other sugar producing countries, would soon reach a magnitude much to be desired.

INTER-PROVINCIAL COAL TRADE.

Reproduced from No. 20 of the Maritime.

The *Coal Trade Review* refers in a late number to the agitation for a duty on coal entering the Dominion, and to the fact that the question affects twelve millions of dollars capital invested in the mines, and a population of 30,000 directly interested in this industry. 　　*　　　*　　　*　　　*　　　*　　　*

The carriage of 200,000 tons of coal at $1 per ton would yield a gross income of $200,000 each open season. Ten iron steam colliers of 1000 tons each, dead weight capacity, would cost in England to-day about £10 per such ton—£100,000 or $500,000 in all.

It is clear, therefore, that at $1 per ton a large profit would accrue to a coal transportation company doing this trade.

We have before us the example of the Philadelphia and Reading Company's steam colliers constructed to enable the company to successfully compete *with other shippers who had a geographical advantage*, such as New York, which is nearer points of heavy consumption ;

Six steamers were built in 1869 and in 1870, the Rattlesnake, Centipede, Achilles, Hercules, Panther and Leopard. The carrying capacity of these vessels ranged from 500 to 1,025 tons.

The first collier completed was the Rattlesnake, and she began operation in June, 1869. She was followed by the Centipede, September, 1869, Achilles, March, 1870, Hercules, May, 1870, Leopard, July, 1870, and Panther in August, 1870.

Many people doubted the wisdom of the collier business, but the officers of the P. & R. R. R. Co. had faith in the ultimate success of the enterprise.

After an experience covering a period of nearly four years i'   )und that the six steamers were not only a success, but that they were totall·   quate to carry on the largely-increased business. In 1874 the tonnage   .od from 4,800 to 16,000 tons. It was, therefore, decided to increase the fi   .nd during the year 1874 the Reading, Harrisburg, Lancaster, Williamsport, Allentown and Pottsville, built by Messrs. Cramp, and the Perkiomen and Berks were added.

The steamers are all built of iron, in the most substantial manner,and with water-tank bottoms. The entire construction is with a view of having the steamers especially adapted to the carrying of coal, as they do not bring any return cargo. The ships are of great strength, so as to enable them to lie aground with a full cargo on board, as they frequently do at the other end of the route.

HOW THE COLLIERS OPERATED.

We have to take Philadelphia as a starting point, and suppose a steamer had been made fast to a pier. The captain finds there a sufficient amount of coal to fill his vessel. The hatches have been opened previous to the vessel coming into the dock. In a very short time the loading commences, and is continued in the quickest way—by shutes in the hold of the vessel. No time is lost in the operations of one of these colliers. They generally leave for their destination at daylight on the day following their arrival here. As soon as the hatches are closed the vessel starts, and the work of cleansing up the decks is performed during the trip down the river. At the place of destination the hour for the arrival of the steamer is known some time before, and where the vessel is moored there is always a small army of men ready to go to work unloading the cargo. No preparations are necessary,as all of the hatches have been opened and other arrangements made before by the crew of the steamer. The unloading is done by means of large buckets,which are filled in the hold and drawn up by machinery at the rate of two or three per minute, and then the coal is dumped into cars and bins, as required. Despatch is the great consideration and one thousand six hundred and fifty tons of coal have been discharged in $11\frac{1}{2}$ working hours. This was at Salem, Mass. At other places the unloading is not done so rapidly. After the discharge of the cargo, water is taken in as ballast, and upon arriving at Port Richmond, Phila., the water is pumped out. The system of running the colliers is very complete. When a steamer reaches its destination the captain telegraphs the hour of his arrival and the hour when he will sail, and by an arrangement of whistle signals, intelligence is obtained at Port Richmond that the vessel is coming up the river, and when she arrives there preparations have already been made for loading her, as has been previously mentioned.

Some of these colliers have at times made trips to almost every port along the coast from Portland to Aspinwall, but the greater portion of the trade is with ports between New York and Portland. The average speed of the steamer is about ten miles per hour.

No time has been lost in the operations of the colliers, and the total number of voyages made in 1877 was 526; miles run, 483,236; coal carried, 602,496 tons. From June, 1860, when the first steamer was run, until the close of 1877, the colliers made 2,107 voyages, ran 2,046,488 miles, and carried 2,099,036 tons of coal.

The expenses of this line for the season, exclusive of insurance, were $337,900 on the carriage of 602,496 tons of coal an average of 900 miles distance, equal to 56 cents per ton, which would be for the distance from Sydney to Toronto, 1,200 miles 75 cents per ton.

The carriage of coal to Toronto from Cleveland, Ohio, is now 80 cents per net ton or 90 cents per ton of 2,240 lbs. The price of Briar Hill is at Cleveland, f. o. b. $3.25, add freight, 80c., $4.05, equal to $4.56 per gross ton at Toronto; the price of Sydney is $2.00 f. o. b., plus freight by Steam Collier, $1.00, would be at Toronto $3.00 per gross ton.

With these facts before us can we refuse to accept as a certainty the inference that, fostered by a protective tariff, our mines would in a very short time be able to organize a system of transport delivery of coal in Ontario for prices far below what any foreign company has done or will do?

————

Extract from the Report of Canal Commissioners Report, 1871.

When Nova Scotia coal of the best description can be supplied abundantly and cheaply to Western Ports, a great impulse will necessarily be given to the transfer of the trade of the St. Lawrence and Lakes to screw steamers, a transfer already taking place, as we have previously shown. A wrong impression prevails in many quarters with respect to the value of Nova Scotia coal, for steam purposes; many think it very inferior to the American article in this particular. The true state of the case, however, is that whenever it has had a fair trial, it answers steam purposes most admirably. The last annual report of the Boston and Yarmouth (N. S.) Steam Navigation Company gives us some important facts bearing upon this subject. In 1868, they had to change the coal used in their boats, in consequence of the strike among the miners of Pennsylvania. Cow Bay, Cape Breton, coal was then burned during the latter part of the season. Fourteen trips were made in which hard coal was used, and eighteen with soft or bituminous. A saving of $1,000 was the result of the eighteen trips. The same steamer has, on the average, consumed forty tons of anthracite per round trip, which, at a cost of $5.50 per ton, made $220. The round trip requires forty-three tons of Cow Bay coal, which at $3.60 per ton is $154.80, showing a saving of $66.20 per trip, or upwards of $2,000 for the season. With a through trade between Toronto and Picton, there is every reason to believe that coal suitable for propellors can be supplied at depots on the lake and river for very little over $4 a ton. With the canals enlarged coal freights would be reduced to the minimum point—a lake propellor would always bring back from the lower ports a cargo of coal, rather than come empty—just as the English timber ships have been accustomed to bring the same article instead of ballast.

EXTRACTS FROM THE REPORT OF THE SELECT COMMITTEE OF THE HOUSE OF COMMONS IN 1877 ON COAL AND INTER-PROVINCIAL TRADE.

WEDNESDAY, April 4th, 1877.

Mr. NAPIER ROBINSON, manager of the Toronto Coal Mining Company, located at Sydney, C.B., examined.

Q. How does the coal compare with the coal from the United States?—It is a better coal in a good many respects than any Ohio coal I have ever seen. The only coal that I would at all compare with it is the Briar Hill, and in point of heating quality and durability our coal is superior to the Briar Hill.

Q. What is your opinion regarding the imposition of a duty on coal imported?—I think it would lead to a very largely extended market.

Q. In what direction?—Both west and in Montreal, Quebec and New Brunswick.

Q. Do you consider the duty would raise or materially affect the price of coal in Ontario?—On the higher grades I don't think think it would affect the price at all. I am sure it would not.

Q. What do you mean by the higher grades?—The higher qualities of bituminous gas coal, and the best domestic coal such as the Briar Hill and Massilon.

By Dr. Tupper :—

Q. Do our coals compare favourably with those of Cleveland for domestic purposes?—Yes. Our coal for domestic purposes is superior to any other coal I have ever seen, and as a steam coal equal to any of them.

By the Chairman :—

Q. You were speaking about the down freights and return cargoes. Do you contemplate or expect that in case of a trade being established with Ontario it would be necessary to consume everything that came down, or is there a port of tranship-ment?—Decidedly we should tranship.

Q. Of what nature would your transhipment be, and to where would they be sent?—There is in the first place a very large port demand; that is, ships calling in at the port of Sydney and taking away an immense quantity of flour, provisions and other articles; and then I think Sydney could be made a port of transhipment for oil and lumber, and to a certain extent, grain for European markets.

Q. Is Sydney much frequented by vessels?—Yes, it is one of the largest ports of call on the Continent. I have frequently seen 20 to 30 vessels arrive there in one day, and 200 and 300 in port at one time.

Q. Why do they come to Sydney?—They come seeking freights.

Q. On account of its situation?—Yes; principally on that account.

WEDNESDAY, 11th April, 1877.

Committee met.

J. M. VERNON, Merchant, called, and made the following statement :—

If a regular trade be carried on between our Maritime Provinces and Ontario, the 50,000 tons of cereals, which now go *via* New York and Boston, would be moved by rail or steamer, and coal could be carried back as return freight, delivered in Toronto at $4.50 long ton. Coal fresh from the mine and delivered by rail is worth 50 cents per ton more than coal that undergoes the dumping process and exposed to the weather in the yards.

The development of our coal fields are of the utmost importance to the country at large, and Ontario is as much interested in this matter as any other Province of the Dominion. But there is no reasonable hope to be indulged in until our iron interests are developed. The iron ores of Canada comprise hematite, limonite, magnitite, &c., &c., equal to any in the world for purity and richness. The magnetic oxide deposits on the Moisic have no superior in the world.

It may be estimated that 4,000,000 of tons of coal would be consumed annually in the Dominion; and under a fair development of home industry, about 300,000 tons of pig iron would be demanded annually. To make this would require the labour of 13,000 men, and the mining of the coal 20,000 men. Thus it is seen that by encouraging these two branches of industry, the labour of 33,000 men are required annually, and which would represent a population of 120,000.

The transportation of this coal and iron alone would double the tonnage of our ports and treble the traffic on our railways, and place us in a position to command the trade of the West and our great North-West which seek other channels to tide-water.

Let the Government extend its fostering care over our national industries, and there is no difficulty in the way of supplying Ontario with Nova Scotia coal for her manufactories and domestic consumption as cheaply, if not cheaper, than she now obtains it from the United States, and much cheaper than the New England States pay for their supply from Virginia and Pennsylvania. New England pays from $6 to $8 per short ton for the coal, and yet she submits gracefully to a 75c. per ton duty because her other industries are amply protected against foreign competition.

Let the Government place us on an equal footing with the United States, by charging them 75 cents duty per short ton, and we will give Ontario as cheap coal as she now receives, and we will be enabled thereby to command our own market, and the $3,320,000 spent annually for coal from other countries will remain at home.

The average cost for five years of the coal imported into Ontario was $4.50 the short ton, or $5 the long ton. Then an arrangement in progress by which Toronto will receive coal at $4.50 the long ton, or about $4 the short ton.

When this coal trade to the West is fully established it will enable railways to carry the products of our Western Provinces to market lower than was ever contemplated by any railway man.

As an illustration of the close relations of the coal trade to the general industry of the country, especially the iron trade, the following calculations may be interesting :—

The Canadian Pacific Railway, from Thunder Bay to the terminus on the Pacific, may be estimated at 2,000 miles. It will require 300,000 tons of pig-iron to make rails, fastenings and bridges, and about 80,000 tons for rolling stock, &c.

To produce this quantity of pig iron will require about 800,000 tons of ore, and 1,200,000 tons of coal. To move this ore and coal, &c., for the purpose of manufacture, will take about 120,000 tons of coal.

The total consumption of coal in making rails, fastenings, iron for bridges, and rolling-stock and for transportation of the same to points of use. &c., cannot fall short of 1,500,000 tons. This quantity could absorb the output of two ordinary mines for ten years, and increase the coal trade of Nova Scotia 150,000 tons for ten years.

It would take two rolling mills ten years to produce the rails and iron ; and the labor required for mining, manufacturing iron, rails, bridges and rolling-stock, and transportation to and fro of all the various articles specified, will be over 3,000 men, representing a population of 15,000 people who would be directly fed and clothed for ten years, by simply developing these sources of wealth as indicated.

Committee met.—Mr. MacKay in the Chair.

Mr. Francis Clemow, Coal Merchant and Director of the Ottawa Gas Company, called and examined:

By Mr. Dymond :—

Has been a Director of the Gas Company for ten years. Trades in both bituminous and anthracite coal. Obtain supplies of bituminous coal from Nova Scotia and the United States. Formerly purchased in Great Britain, but has discontinued since 1873, owing to the advance in price. Buys chiefly from the Caledonia Block House, Intercolonial and International Mines. Uses 3,000 tons of gas coal per annum. That is the highest quality of coal, and cost last year $5.75 per ton of 2,240 pounds. The cost was made up as follows : Initial cost, $2; freight to Montreal, $2; harbour dues, 10 cents per net ton; insurance, 3 cents per ton; freight to Ottawa $1.60—total, $5.75. This year was offered coal at the mines above named for $1.50; freight to Montreal, $2; harbour dues, &c., 13 cents; freight to Ottawa, $1.50—total, $5.15 per gross ton. Has bought the Willow Bank, United States, coal, last year, at $5 per net ton, and the Youghoigheny at $5.90; in both cases the charges included delivery on the wharf at Ottawa. At the above rate American coal would come to $5.62½ for Willow Bank and $6.64 for Youghoigheny.

By Mr. Tupper :—

Mr. G. H. Dobson called and examined :

Q. Where do you reside ?—In Sydney, Cape Breton.

Q. Were you sent as a delegate to the Dominion Board of Trade ?—Yes.

Q. By whom ?—By the Cape Breton Board of Trade.

Q. Have you been spending some considerable time in endeavoring to ascertain how far trade can be promoted between the Upper Provinces and Nova Scotia ?—Yes ; for one year.

Q. You have devoted your attention principally to that ?—Yes.

Q. Are you engaged in that way now ?—Yes.

Q. What is the annual consumption of coal in Canada?—Last year it was 1,415,516 tons, of which 352,414 tons was hard coal, I think. There is a little difference in our imports being made up to the 30th of June and the production by the mines return being made up to the 31st December.

Q. Where is the natural market of the Nova Scotia coal ?—Wherever we can get a return cargo from, or get a vessel bound to a loading port. It has been stated here, by previous witnesses, that the natural market for Nova Scotia coal is the New England States; but so far as I can see, we have no particular natural market. England sends coal all over the world, and wherever there is a demand, and we can get vessels for, is our natural market. I have been engaged in the trade for eight years, and I should say that Montreal and Quebec are as convenient markets for us as the United States.

Q. Would the securing of the Canadian markets benefit the coal owners and trade generally ?—Yes.

Q. How ?—It would give our coal producers the supplying of the Canadian markets; and would also give the Canadian producers the supplying of the Maritime Provinces. I might state that, last year the Maritime Provinces, inclusive of Newfoundland, imported 463,586 barrels of flour and 9,254,273 pounds of meat from the United States.

Q. In what year was the coal trade most prosperous ?—In 1873.

Q. How many tons was produced that year ?—1,051,467 tons.

Q. How many men were employed ?—5,000 men and boys, representing a population of 30,000.

Q. How many days' work did they do in the aggregate ?—955,722 days' work.

Q. How many vessels were there employed in carrying the coal, and what was their tonnage ?—3,604 vessels, of which 428 were steamers, representing a gross tonnage of 820,144 tons.

Q. How many seamen did they employ ?—About 22,000.

Q. What amount of capital was there in circulation, directly and indirectly caused by the coal production ?—The best estimate I can get places the amount at $4,913,381.

Q. How do you propose to send coal to Ontario ?—By securing the markets of the Maritime Provinces for Ontario products, and the Ontario markets for our coal we now import largely from the United States; last year our imports from the United States aggregated $7,622,712.

Q. Those products, you say, could be largely obtained from Old Canada if an interchange could be made between them and Nova Scotia coal ?—Yes, very largely; I find that the coal imports into Canada are estimated at $3,220,300.

Q. How are the Nova Scotia coal mines situated with regard to supplying the Canadian market ?—Very conveniently. We are half-way between the grain-producing centres of the West, and the market of the Old World—halfway between Chicago and Liverpool. The lake vessels might terminate their voyage at Sydney, and their cargoes be there transhipped into the ocean vessels. I may say that Atlantic freights are less by 30 per cent. from Sydney than from New York, Baltimore and other American ports; and, besides, the port charges at Sydney are $100, against from $800 to $1,000 at Montreal and the American ports.

Q. Does England supply distant markets with coal, as near to them as the American mines are to Ontario?—Yes. For instance, she supplies Cuba, that has American coal quite near, and San Francisco, with British Columbia coal near. Coals are shipped 15,000 miles to India, which are quite near to the China and Australian coalfields.

By Mr. Goudge:—

Q. On what do you base your statement that the ocean freights from Sydney are 30 per cent. lower than those from the more southerly ports?—On the fact that we have been tendered vessels by shipowners in New Brunswick and Nova Scotia at 30 per cent. less from Sydney than from the other ports.

Q. Why do you get them for 30 per cent. less?—The reason is that we are 800 miles nearer Europe than New York and other American ports, and the port charges are very much less.

Q. Does Newfoundland take flour from the United States?—Yes.

Q. In case a large coal trade existed between Ontario and Nova Scotia, could Ontario supply the Newfoundland market?—Canada could supply the Newfoundland market with flour with return cargoes of coal west from Nova Scotia. Mr. Robinson in his evidence alluded to the vessels going out from England and bringing coal as ballast. I think there are only five ports in England from which vessels take coal. It does not pay the vessels to change ports and bring out coal as ballast, nor can the English coal producer supply coal as ballast where they have to ship it to ports where vessels are lying. I hold that Montreal and Quebec would get more tonnage by taking coal from Sydney, than if they were dependent on English coal as ballast. Sydney is becoming the North American port of call, and vessels bound west seeking freights call there now almost entirely. On arrival they enquire for Montreal, St. John, New York, Baltimore and Philadelphia freight markets, and often Montreal quotes higher than any of the other ports; and could we get coal freights at a low rate to Montreal Montreal would command more ocean tonnage.

Q. That is if you prevented vessels from bringing out coal as ballast?—We could furnish coal as cheaply as the English coal and could give Montreal and Quebec more tonnage.

EFFECT OF THE COAL DUTY.

In 1870 the Parliament of Canada imposed a duty of 50 cents per ton on all imported coal and removed it in 1871, with the following result:—

Imports in 1869,—389,485, the year before the duty.
    do   1870,—272,595, the year of the duty.
    do   1871,—484,826, the year after the duty.
Cost to the consumer in Montreal, in 1869, $5 to $8 per ton.
        do   1870, $4.50   do
        do   1871, $5 to $10   do
Productions in Nova Scotia, 1869, 511,795.
        do   1870, 568,277.
        do   1871, 596,418.

We thus see that while the duty in no way increased the price of coal to the consumer, it yet diminished our imports to the extent of 116,890, and enabled the Nova Scotia collieries to increase their shipments by 56,482.

Table of distances from Sydney to the following ports:—

		Miles.	Depth of Water.	
Sydney to	Quebec	720	...	
do	Montreal	900	21	feet.
do	Toronto	1,200	13	do
do	Chicago	2,161	14	do
do	Miramichi	300	21	do
do	St. John's, Newfoundland	400	...	
do	St. John, N.B.	540	...	
do	Halifax, N.S.	240	...	
do	Portland, U.S.	580	..	
do	Boston, U.S.	600	..	
do	New York, U.S.	750	..	

INTERPROVINCIAL TRADE.

Shipments from Quebec and Ontario to the Lower Provinces *via* the Intercolonial Railway for 1878:—

Barrels of flour	637,778
Bushels of grain.	531,170
Head of live stock	48,498
All other goods in tons	375,025

Shipments from Montreal to Lower Provinces. *via* the River St. Lawrence, for 1878:—

Flour in barrels	161,885
Meal do	6,345
Butter	9,812
Cheese in boxes	2,054
Pork in barrels.	5,765
Lard do	62
Wheat in bushels	4,751
Other grain do	13,000